THE COUNTRYSIDE

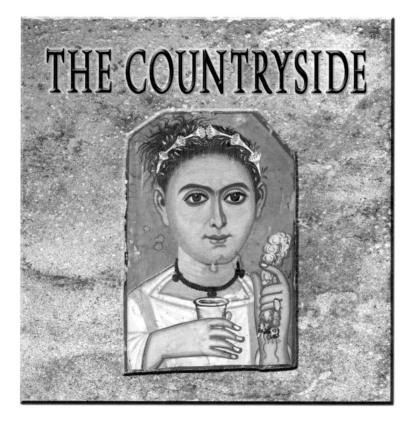

LIFE IN THE ROMAN EMPIRE

THE COUNTRYSIDE

BY

KATHRYN HINDS

BENCHMARK BOOKS

MARSHALL CAVENDISH
NEW YORK

To Helen Bacon,
Professor of Classics (retired), Barnard College
Pro introductione linguae latinae, gratia magna.

The author and publisher wish to specially thank J. Brett McClain
of the Oriental Institute of the University of Chicago
for his invaluable help in reading the manuscript.

❧

Benchmark Books Marshall Cavendish 99 White Plains Road Tarrytown, New York 10591-9001
www.marshallcavendish.com Copyright © 2005 by Marshall Cavendish Corporation All rights
reserved. No part of this book may be reproduced or utilized in any form or by any means electronic
or mechanical including photocopying, recording, or by any information storage and retrieval
system, without permission from the copyright holders. All Internet sites were available and accurate
when this book was sent to press. Book design by Michael Nelson LIBRARY OF CONGRESS
CATALOGING-IN-PUBLICATION DATA: Hinds, Kathryn, 1962- The countryside / by Kathryn Hinds.
p. cm. — (Life in the Roman empire) Includes bibliographical references and index.
ISBN 0-7614-1656-0 1. Rome—Social life and customs—Juvenile literature. 2. Country life—
Rome—Juvenile literature. I. Title II. Series: Hinds, Kathryn, 1962- . Life in the Roman empire.
DG78.H5536 2005 937′.009734—dc22 2004009496

Art Research: Rose Corbett Gordon, Mystic CT
Front cover (top): Scala/Art Resource, NY; (bottom): Musée des Antiquités Nationales, St-Germain-en-Laye,
France/Lauros/Giraudon/Bridgeman Art Library Back cover: Erich Lessing/Art Resource, NY
Page i: Brooklyn Museum of Art, New York/Charles Edwin Wilbour Fund/Bridgeman Art Library;
page iii: Santa Costanza, Rome/Bridgeman Art Library; pages vi, 15, 58: The Art Archive / Dagli Orti;
page viii: The Art Archive / Byzantine Mosaic Museum Istanbul / Dagli Orti; pages 3, 56: The Art
Archive / Museo della Civilta Romana, Rome / Dagli Orti; pages 5, 8, 35, 40, 57: Erich Lessing/Art
Resource, NY; pages 10, 28: Gilles Mermet/Art Resource, NY; page13: Musée National du Bardo,
Le Bardo, Tunisia/Lauros/Giraudon/Bridgeman Art Library; page 16: Rome/Index/Bridgeman Art
Library; page18: Archivo Iconografico, S.A./Corbis; pages 22, 32, 61: Scala/Art Resource, NY; pages
24, 49: The Granger Collection, New York; page 25: Villa Romana del Casale, Piazza Armerina,
Sicily/Bridgeman Art Library; pages 26, 46: The Art Archive / Archaeological Museum Naples / Dagli
Orti; page 31: The Art Archive / Archaeological Museum Tipasa Algeria / Dagli Orti; page 33: Musée
des Antiquités Nationales, St-Germain-en-Laye, France/Lauros/Giraudon/Bridgeman Art Library;
page 36: Pushkin Museum, Moscow/Bridgeman Art Library; page 39: Ashmoleon Museum,
Oxford/Bridgeman Art Library; page 44: Gaziantep Archaeological Museum, Gaziantep,
Turkey/Bridgeman Art Library; page 47: The Art Archive / Archaeological Museum Naples / Dagli
Orti; page 50: The Stapleton Collection/Bridgeman Art Library; page 52: Mimmo Jodice/Corbis;
page 54: Alinari Archives/Corbis; page 63: Museum fur Vor und Fruhgeschichte, Saarbrucken,
Germany/Bridgeman Art Library

Printed in China
1 3 5 6 4 2

front cover: Mosaics showing various farm tasks: feeding animals, picking fruit, plowing,
preparing storage jars, and harvesting grapes
back cover: A child goes for a ride in his miniature chariot.
half-title page: A boy decked out for a festive occasion in Roman-ruled Egypt
title page: Two young farmworkers haul away a cartload of newly harvested grapes.
About the Roman Empire, p. vi: A bird hunt in the Italian countryside

CONTENTS

ABOUT THE ROMAN EMPIRE VI

I. THE EMPIRE'S SUPPORT SYSTEM 1

II. COUNTRY COMMUNITIES 11

III. COUNTRY HOMES 19

IV. WORKING THE LAND 29

V. MEN OF THE SOIL 37

VI. RURAL WOMEN 45

VII. GROWING UP IN THE COUNTRYSIDE 53

VIII. HARD TIMES AND HOLIDAYS 59

GLOSSARY 64

FOR FURTHER READING 65

ONLINE INFORMATION 65

BIBLIOGRAPHY 66

SOURCES FOR QUOTATIONS 67

INDEX 70

ABOUT THE ROMAN EMPIRE

When we think about the Roman Empire, we often picture gladiators, chariot races, togas, marble statues, and legions on the march. These images tell only part of the story of ancient Rome. According to the Romans themselves, their city was founded in 753 B.C.E.* At first Rome was a kingdom, then it became a republic. In 27 B.C.E. Augustus Caesar became Rome's absolute ruler—its emperor. Meanwhile, this city built on seven hills overlooking the Tiber River had been steadily expanding its power. In Augustus's time Rome controlled all of Italy and the rest of mainland Europe west of the Rhine River and south of the Danube River, as well as much of North Africa and the Middle East.

At its height, the Roman Empire reached all the way from Britain to Persia. It brought together an array of European, African, and Middle Eastern peoples, forming a vibrant multicultural society. During much of the empire's existence, its various ethnic and religious groups got along with remarkable tolerance and understanding—a model that can still inspire us today. We can also be inspired by the Romans' tremendous achievements in the arts, architecture, literature, law, and philosophy, just as they have inspired and influenced people in Europe and the Americas for hundreds of years.

So step back in time, and visit the empire at its most powerful, from 27 B.C.E. to around 200 C.E. In this book you will meet farmers, slaves, soldiers, poets, and others who lived and worked in the rural areas ruled by Rome. These people had many of the same joys and sorrows, hopes and fears that we do, but their world was very different from ours. Forget about telephones, computers, cars, and televisions, and imagine what it might have been like to live among the people who ruled much of the ancient world. Welcome to life in the Roman Empire. . . .

* A variety of systems of dating have been used by different cultures throughout history. Many historians now prefer to use B.C.E. (Before Common Era) and C.E. (Common Era) instead of B.C. (Before Christ) and A.D. (Anno Domini), out of respect for the diversity of the world's peoples. In this book, all dates are C.E. unless otherwise noted.

I

THE EMPIRE'S SUPPORT SYSTEM

THEN LET ME LOVE THE COUNTRY, THE RIVERS RUNNING
THROUGH VALLEYS, THE STREAMS AND WOODLANDS. . . .
GIVE ME BROAD FIELDS AND SWEEPING RIVERS,
LOFTY MOUNTAIN RANGES IN DISTANT LANDS,
COLD PRECIPITOUS VALLEYS, WHERE I MAY LIE BENEATH
THE ENORMOUS DARKNESS OF THE BRANCHES!
—VIRGIL, *GEORGICS*

 hen we think about ancient Rome, we usually picture life in the great city itself, and in all the other cities of the empire. Roman civilization was focused on urban life—even the word "civilization" comes from one of the Romans' words for "city," *civis*. Most people in the Roman Empire, however, did not live in cities. They lived in rural areas: on scattered farmsteads, in villages and small towns, or on plantation-like farming estates. Although history has largely ignored these people, their work as farmers, herders, spinners, weavers—among other rural occupations—was essential to the strength and well-being of the Roman Empire.

opposite:
A country dweller carries chickens and a basket of eggs to a town market.

1

A ROMAN IDEAL

According to legend, the founder of Rome was Romulus, a shepherd. Many of his followers were shepherds, too, and farmers. The early city, in fact, was a union of farming villages scattered over seven neighboring hills. Even after Rome was well on its way to becoming the greatest city on the Italian peninsula, the Romans thought of themselves as a nation of simple, honest, hard-working farmers. After Augustus came to power, and Rome dominated the Mediterranean world, Romans still looked back with pride on their rural traditions. As the great poet Virgil wrote of this heritage, "through this, Rome became the fairest thing on earth."

The countryside and rural life were celebrated not only by Virgil but by many other poets, including Horace, Tibullus, and Martial. The authors Varro and Columella composed treatises on agriculture. Author-statesman Pliny the Younger often wrote about his enjoyment of his country villas and his concerns about his farming estates. The historian Tacitus was one of many Romans who felt that society had become too "citified"—overly sophisticated, even decadent—and looked back on the "good old days" of the rural past. Horace, for example, says this about the great Romans of former times:

> Those were the sons of farmers and soldiers too—
> tough males, accustomed, mattock in hand, to break
> > hard clods, and bring home logs for firing
> > under the eye of a mother stern and
> strong-willed. . . .

Such authors—nearly all wealthy men who lived, at least part-time, in the city—idealized country life. Unfortunately, we have very

HAPPINESS IN THE COUNTRYSIDE

Publius Vergilius Maro, known in English as Virgil or Vergil, lived from 70 to 19 B.C.E. Ever since his death, he has been regarded as the greatest of all Roman poets. He was born in a small village in northern Italy, but lived for some years in Rome, where he became acquainted with the emperor Augustus. Virgil always retained a love for the countryside, however, and a respect for farmers, although he sometimes idealized their lives. Following is a selection from one of his *Georgics*, a group of poems he wrote about rural life.

> Happy—even too happy, if they knew their bliss—
> are farmers, who receive, far from the clash of war,
> an easy livelihood from the just and generous earth.
> Although they own no lofty mansion with proud gates,
> from every hall disgorging floods of visitors, . . .
> still they sleep without care and live without deceit,
> rich with various plenty, peaceful in broad expanses,
> in grottoes, lakes of living water, cool dark glens,
> with the brute music of cattle, soft sleep at noon
> beneath the trees: they have forests, the lairs of wild game;
> they have sturdy sons, hard-working, content with little,
> the sanctity of God, and reverence for the old.
> Justice, quitting this earth, left her last footprints there.

little written material from the common people whose lives centered on farming and other rural work. Few of these people knew how to read and write, and most of them worked too long and hard to take time for recording their experiences. Once in a while, though, we do hear the voice of someone from the countryside, as in this inscription from the tombstone of a North African man:

> From the day of my birth I have lived by working my land; neither my land nor I has ever had a rest. . . . Twelve years' harvests I cut under the raging sun, . . . and for eleven years I commanded teams of harvesters. . . . Hard work, and contentment with little, finally brought me a home with a farmstead, and my home lacks nothing in wealth. Furthermore, my career has achieved the rewards of office; . . . from a poor farm boy I actually became a censor [an official in the local government]. I have seen my children and my grandchildren grow up around me, and I have enjoyed years distinguished by the merits of my career. . . . Thus has he deserved to die who has lived honourably.

SUSTAINING THE CITY

In the ancient world, country and city generally had a very close relationship. Most cities controlled outlying rural areas, which depended on the cities for protection and supplied them with grain, vegetables, honey, wool, and other agricultural products. Usually there were many people who lived in cities but left them each day to work in the nearby fields. In numerous cases, there were fields, orchards, and pastures even within city walls.

Rome itself, with more than a million people, was so large that

Hunters load a deer and an ostrich onto a ship for transport to Rome.

the surrounding region could not support it alone. More than six million sacks of grain a year were required to feed the city's residents. This grain was grown mainly in Sicily, Egypt, and other parts of North Africa. North Africa was also home to extensive olive orchards, as was Spain. Rome imported olive oil from both regions to meet the needs of its population. The oil was used in everything from cooking to lamp fuel, to soaps and body lotions. Wine was another item exported from Spain to Rome in great quantity. Some of the best wines enjoyed by upper-class Romans, however, were produced in the vineyards scattered over the Italian countryside. Most of the pork and wool used in Rome came from the province of Cisalpine Gaul, the region of Italy just south of the Alps.

All over the empire, products flowed into cities from rural areas. The countryside provided a wide array of goods, from meat and milk to linen and dyestuffs to precious metals and building materials. Numerous cities, especially in the eastern empire, were as dependent on imported grain as Rome was. In many of these places, the surrounding region easily could have produced grain—but instead the land was used for the more profitable crops of grapes and olives. Basic food supplies often had to travel a long distance from country to city.

Another way in which the countryside played a supporting role to cities was by providing a place where busy urbanites could relax and "get away from it all" for a time. As Martial wrote, "Do you ask why I often make for my little farm in arid Nomentum [a small town northeast of Rome], and the untidy household of my villa? In the city . . . poor men have no place where they can think or stay quiet. . . . Whenever I'm worn out with anxiety, and want to sleep, I go to my farm." Rome (like other Mediterranean cities) was not only noisy and bustling, but in the summer it could be unbearably hot, so wealthy people migrated to villas in the hills or near the sea. Many villas were not simply "vacation homes" for their owners but were part of working farms. Agricultural products and the money from their sale were, in fact, the main source of wealth for many upper-class Romans.

CONQUERED COUNTRYSIDE

Rome was the mightiest military power in the Western world. Its conquests gave it control over numerous diverse areas. Some parts of the empire were thickly urbanized, such as Italy, Greece, southern Spain, and the coasts of Asia Minor. Other provinces were far more rural, particularly in the north and west, with cities fewer and farther between. It was in these less urbanized areas, generally speaking, that the bulk of Rome's troops were stationed.

The Roman army had two main divisions, the legions and the auxiliaries. Legionary soldiers were all Roman citizens, mostly from Italy and what are now Spain, southern France, and Turkey. The auxiliaries were soldiers recruited from the provinces. Some were citizens, but most earned Roman citizenship at the completion of their military service. The majority of legionaries were foot soldiers, while auxiliaries often had specialized skills, such as fighting on horseback or using bows or slings. Some auxiliary units were made up of men required to fight for Rome as part of a treaty agreement between their people and the empire. In any case, up until about the middle of the second century, auxiliaries rarely served in their home province. So, for example, the soldiers who kept order for the empire in Britain were from what are now the Netherlands, northeastern Greece, Algeria, and Ukraine. When auxiliaries and legionaries were discharged from the army, they often settled in towns or farming communities in the province where they were stationed. This was one of the most important ways that Roman culture spread through the countryside of conquered territories.

Roman rule brought order and peace to conquered areas, but at a price. Many thought this price was too high, although few had the courage to speak out. Roman soldiers were never far away, ready to deal with troublemakers at a moment's notice. But in the 80s C.E., the empire met strong resistance when it tried to push its rule into northern Britain. The historian Tacitus put the following speech

A warrior north of the empire's frontier defends his home from a Roman soldier.

into the mouth of a British leader named Calgacus, rallying his warriors against the Romans in what is now northeastern Scotland:

Up until this day, we who live in this last strip of land and last home of liberty have been protected by our very remoteness. . . . But now the farthest limits of Britain have been opened up. . . . Beyond us, there are no tribes, nothing except waves and rocks and, more dangerous than these, the Romans, whose oppression you have in vain tried to escape by obedience and submission. Plunderers of the world they are, and now that there is no more territory left to occupy their hands which have already laid the world waste, they are scouring the seas. If the enemy is rich, they are greedy; if the enemy is poor, they are power-hungry. . . . Alone of all men they covet rich nations and poor nations with equal passion. They rob, they slaughter, they plunder—and they call it 'empire.' Where they make a waste-land, they call it 'peace.'

Nature has planned that each man love his children and family very dearly. Yet these are torn from us . . . to be slaves elsewhere. . . . Our possessions and our money are consumed in providing tribute; our farmland and our yearly produce are consumed in providing them with grain; our very bodies and hands are worn down while clearing forests and swamps for them, who beat and insult us.

·II·

COUNTRY COMMUNITIES

HAIL, EARTHLY PARADISE, MIGHTY MOTHER OF CROPS
AND MOTHER OF MEN!
—VIRGIL PRAISING ITALY IN THE *GEORGICS*

here was great diversity in the Roman Empire. This applied not only to people and their customs but also to their environments and natural resources. Britain was damp and chilly, North Africa hot and dry. Germany was heavily wooded; in Greece the terrain was rough and rocky. Along the Nile River in Egypt, the flat, fertile land was perfect for growing wheat; Italian hillsides were covered with grapevines and olive trees. In Spain the earth held rich deposits of gold and other metals, while marble could be quarried from many parts of Asia Minor.

How people lived in the countryside naturally depended on climate, the quality of the land, and the available resources. We also need to remember that a great deal of change has occurred since

opposite:
A wealthy woman, surrounded by servants, enjoys the garden at her villa in North Africa.

Rome ruled the Mediterranean world. For example, forests covered much more of western Europe in Roman times than today, and areas in North Africa that are now desert were then green with orchards of olive trees.

A VARIETY OF VILLAGES

Many country people lived in villages. Some rural settlements might have only a handful of houses, occupied by farm families that worked the surrounding fields. Other villages might be home not only to farmers but also to craftspeople, and there might be an inn and other amenities. Pliny mentioned in a letter to one of his friends that the village near his seaside villa had three public bathhouses.

Small towns were also important to the countryside. Farmers could sell some of their produce at markets in these towns and could use the money to buy things that they couldn't make themselves or get from village craftspeople. Virgil gave this description of a country dweller's visit to his local market town: "Often the farmer drives the sluggish donkey, loading its sides with oil or cheap apples, while on the return trip he brings back from town a grooved millstone or a lump of dark pitch."

In much of the Roman Empire, villages were often made up entirely of native people living in their traditional ways. For instance, the first four books of the New Testament of the Bible frequently describe village life in the province of Judaea (roughly, modern Israel), where fishing was an important part of the rural economy. Throughout the empire, there could be a good deal of variety even in the basic layout of country communities: as an example, many British villages were surrounded by wide ditches, while North African villages were often walled and fortified with towers.

LIFE ON THE EMPIRE'S FRINGES

In mainland Europe, the Roman Empire's northern boundary was the Danube River. Across it lived a number of Germanic tribes. Rome tried many times to conquer German territory, but even when it succeeded, these lands were hard to hold on to. Only in the west, along the Rhine River, did the empire manage to maintain a presence in Germany. This area was a military zone for many years, then in 90 C.E. became the provinces of Upper and Lower Germany. Not long afterward, Tacitus wrote his *Germania,* a study of the lands and peoples of the Rhine-Danube region. Here is an excerpt, in which Tacitus describes the Germans' typical communities:

It is well known that none of the German tribes live in cities, that even individually they do not permit houses to touch each other: they live separated and scattered, according as spring-water, meadow, or grove appeals to each man: they lay out their villages not, after our fashion, with buildings contiguous [touching each other] and connected; every one keeps a clear space round his house, whether it be a precaution against the chances of fire, or just ignorance of building. They have not even learned to use quarry-stone or tiles: the timber they use for all purposes is unshaped, and stops short of all ornament or attraction: certain buildings are smeared with a stucco bright and glittering enough to be a substitute for paint and frescoes. . . .

Land is taken up by a village as a whole, in quantity according to the number of the cultivators: they then distribute it among themselves on the basis of rank, such distribution being made easy by the extent of domain occupied. They change the arable land yearly, and there is still land to spare, for they do not strain the fertility and resources of the soil. . . . Grain is the only harvest required of the land; accordingly the year itself is not divided into as many parts as with us: winter, spring, summer have a meaning and name; of autumn the name alike and bounties are unknown.

GREAT ESTATES

In both Italy and the provinces, large tracts of land were owned by the emperor—and all of Egypt belonged to him. Each of the emperor's estates was run by an official called a procurator, who was often a freed slave. The procurator usually rented out parts of the estate to tenant farmers. Sometimes extensive parcels of land were rented to one person. This "lessee-in-chief" or chief tenant would be allowed to have part of the estate farmed for himself, and he would sublet the rest to humbler tenant farmers. The emperor's estates often incorporated entire villages, as this inscription from North Africa shows:

> Anyone living within the estate of Villa Magna Variana, that is, in the village of Siga, is permitted to bring those fields which are unsurveyed under cultivation. . . . Of the crops produced on such land they [the tenants] must in accordance with the Mancian Law deliver shares . . . to the chief lessees or bailiffs of this estate as follows. . . . one third of the wheat from the threshing floor, one third of the barley from the threshing floor, one fourth of the beans from the threshing floor, one third of the wine from the vat, one third of the oil extracted, one *sextarius* [a little more than a pint] of honey per hive.

Other wealthy Romans also had great landholdings—it is said that at one point, half the province of Africa (roughly, modern Tunisia) was owned by six men. This was an extreme case, however, and most estates were not so vast. Large landowners generally lived in the cities, not on their estates. But on most estates they would

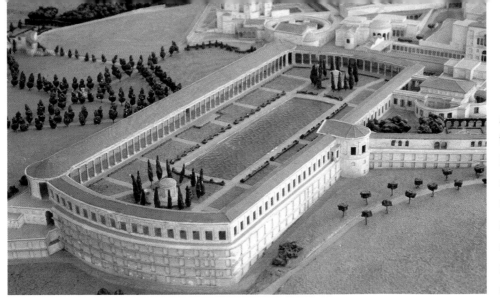

A portion of the emperor Hadrian's magnificent country estate at Tivoli (fifteen miles outside Rome), reconstructed in a scale model

have a villa, which they visited from time to time. Many wealthy Romans had a network of villas throughout Italy, so that they and their friends would have places to stay while traveling, since there were few decent hotels. The estates themselves were run by stewards or bailiffs and worked by slaves, tenant farmers, sharecroppers, or some combination of these. Italian estates produced mainly wine, olive oil, and grain, but in some parts of the peninsula great tracts of land were devoted to cattle ranching.

The poet Horace had a fairly modest estate, about thirty miles from Rome. He spent as much time in his villa there as he could—"I always leave with a sigh whenever loathsome business drags me back to Rome," he wrote. He rented part of his estate to five tenant farmers, each family living in its own cottage and working a plot of land. The rest of the estate was worked by eight slaves, overseen by a foreman. Its produce (including the profits from sales) directly supported the poet. He had grain fields, a vegetable garden, an orchard, a vineyard, an olive grove, a wood, pastureland, and cattle, sheep, and goats. The countryside around Horace's estate was still quite wild: once while rambling alone in the forest, he unexpectedly came upon a wolf—luckily for both, the poet was unarmed, and the wolf soon went its own way.

FRONTIER FORTS

Roman legions were headquartered in leading provincial cities. Soldiers, however—both legionaries and auxiliaries—manned outposts and forts that were strung through the countryside or along the empire's boundaries. One such frontier was Hadrian's Wall, which divided the province of Britannia (Britain) from what is now Scotland. Built into the wall were sixteen or seventeen fortresses, each manned by some five hundred auxiliaries. There were also watchtowers every third of a mile and fortified gateways, called milecastles, roughly every mile. Each milecastle could house a garrison of around thirty men.

Wherever soldiers were stationed, villages soon came into being. Some local people wanted the protection of the Roman soldiers, for in many places bandits and raiders threatened the safety of the countryside. Others were more interested in earning money

Roman soldiers building a fortified camp during the course of the emperor Trajan's war to conquer Dacia (modern Romania)

by supplying the soldiers with goods and services. Until 197 C.E. rank-and-file legionaries and auxiliaries were not allowed to marry, but often they had unofficial wives who, with their children, naturally wanted to live as close to the army camp as possible. So a typical settlement near a military base might include a tavern, a few craftspeople's workshops, a marketplace, and the homes of soldiers' families and of people who farmed the surrounding countryside. Over time, many such settlements grew into full-fledged towns and cities.

Not all rural people, however, lived in villages, on villas, or near military posts. In almost every province there were at least some freeholders who occupied scattered or isolated farmsteads, working land that often had been passed down through families for generations. And in North Africa and a few other areas on the empire's edges, many groups carried on an age-old nomadic lifestyle. They traveled from place to place, following the grazing patterns of their animals. At the same time they played a role in village culture by trading products from their herds for grain, vegetables, and the like. In addition, nomads provided temporary, seasonal labor on many farms.

·III·
COUNTRY HOMES

IF WE MUST LIVE IN PERFECT HARMONY WITH NATURE
AND FIRST DISCOVER A SITE ON WHICH TO BUILD OUR HOME,
WHAT PLACE IS BETTER THAN THE HEAVENLY COUNTRYSIDE?
—HORACE, *EPISTLES*

ural people lived in various ways in different parts of the empire. This can be seen in housing, artwork, religious practices, and clothing. For example, peasant men in Britain and Germany often wore woolen breeches and hooded hip-length cloaks that fastened up the front. Male North African farmworkers, in contrast, wore lightweight tunics that reached to just above their knees. In Syria, the traditional dress included baggy trousers that fitted closely at the ankles. The poet Ovid described some of the semi-nomadic men who lived near the mouth of the Danube this way: "With [animal] skins and loose breeches they keep off the evils of the cold; their shaggy faces are protected with long locks." These men's long hair and beards contrasted sharply with the short hair and clean-shaven faces generally favored in Italy by town dwellers and country folk alike.

opposite:
A home on the bank of the Nile River in Roman-ruled Egypt

19

HUMBLE ABODES

The architect Vitruvius noted that the native people in different parts of the empire each had traditional building styles. Houses in what are now France and Spain, he said, were roofed with oak shingles or thatch. On the south coast of the Black Sea, tall log cabins were typical. "On the other hand," Vitruvius continued,

> the Phrygians [of central Asia Minor], who live in an open country, have no forests and consequently lack timber. They therefore select a natural hillock, run a trench through the middle of it, dig passages, and extend the interior space as widely as the site admits. Over it they build a pyramidal roof of logs fastened together, and this they cover with reeds and brushwood, heaping up very high mounds of earth above their dwellings. Thus their fashion in houses makes their winters very warm and their summers very cool.

We know from other evidence that British houses were often round and constructed of wattle and daub, with steep, conical thatched roofs. Egyptian villagers built their homes of mud brick, with flat roofs. The Romans rarely interfered with these various building traditions, but in their own settlements, whether in Italy or the provinces, they built in their own style.

Roman country houses were mainly rectangular in shape. They might be constructed of stone, wood, concrete with a brick facing, or a combination of these materials. Roofs were usually covered with clay tiles. The poorest homes had floors of hard-packed earth; people who were more comfortably off had wood, stone, or tile underfoot. Walls were often plastered or whitewashed inside and out.

A simple home or cottage was typically partitioned into a few small rooms, one leading into another. Archaeologists in Italy have found the remains of a humble farmhouse with an interior measuring approximately thirty-three feet by fifteen feet. There is evidence that farm animals sheltered in one part of the house—a common living arrangement in many places in the past. The animals were protected from thieves and the weather, and when it was cold, their body heat helped warm the house for the human residents.

The majority of country people had only a few simple furnishings: at most probably a bed or couch, a storage chest, a table, a bench or two, a cupboard, some large clay storage jars, and a hand-mill for grinding grain. The kitchen area had a raised open hearth and, sometimes, an oven. To cook over the hearth fire, people would use a griddle, a spit for roasting meat (when it was available), and in some areas a cauldron hung on a tripod. In a small cottage, the hearth fire was the only source of heat. It also created a lot of smoke, which escaped through an open door or window, or through holes in the roof. Windows could be closed with wooden shutters, or may have been covered with oiled paper or a thin sheet of animal skin. The only artificial light came from oil lamps or, in areas that did not raise olives, candles made of beeswax or animal fat.

On most farms, there would be other buildings in addition to the house. The number and type of outbuildings depended on how well-off the family was and what they were raising. If the farm was prosperous, there could be a separate structure for the kitchen, a bathhouse, workshops for making olive oil and wine, storage buildings, and stables. Many such farms were arranged around a rectangular farmyard, with the house on one side and the additional buildings set along two other sides.

ᘐ COUNTRY HOSPITALITY ᘏ

On an everyday basis, most country people ate porridge, beans, occasionally a little pork, and probably some seasonal fruits and vegetables. The following passage from Ovid's long poem *Metamorphoses* describes a special-occasion meal (which would be easy to make today) and also gives several interesting details about how country people lived. In the selection, Baucis and Philemon, an elderly rural couple, are visited by two mysterious travelers. The old woman and man are poor, and they don't realize that their visitors are gods in disguise, but all the same they treat them with generous hospitality.

> So, when the gods came to this little cottage,
> Ducking their heads to enter, the old man
> Pulled out a rustic bench for them to rest on,
> As Baucis spread a homespun cover for it,
> And then she poked the ashes around a little,
> Still warm from last night's fire, and got them going . . .
>   . . . and then she took the cabbage
> Her man had brought from the well-watered garden,
> And stripped the outer leaves off. And Philemon
> Reached up, with a forked stick, for the side of bacon,

That hung below the smoky beam, and cut it,
Saved up so long, a fair-sized chunk, and dumped it
In the boiling water. They made conversation
To keep the time from being too long, and brought
A couch with willow frame and feet, and on it
They put a sedge-grass mattress. . . .
Baucis, her skirts tucked up, was setting the table
With trembling hands. One table-leg was wobbly;
A piece of shell fixed that. She scoured the table,
Made level now, with a handful of green mint,
Put on the olives, black or green, and cherries
Preserved in dregs of wine, endive and radish,
And cottage cheese, and eggs, turned over lightly
In the warm ash, with shells unbroken. The dishes
Of course, were earthenware . . .

                        . . . and the goblets
Were beech, the inside coated with yellow wax.
No time at all, and the warm food was ready,
And wine brought out, of no particular vintage,
And pretty soon they had to clear the table
For the second course; here there were nuts and figs
And dates and plums and apples in wide baskets—
Remember how apples smell?—and purple grapes
Fresh from the vines, and a white honeycomb
As centerpiece, and all around the table
Shone kindly faces, nothing mean or poor
Or skimpy in good will.

RURAL RETREATS

Although Horace once claimed, "In a poor cottage you may live a better life than kings and the friends of kings," his own country home was far from a cottage. Archaeologists have been exploring the site and the remains of Horace's villa for many years. Together with a large formal garden, it took up an area roughly the size of a football field. The entrance led directly into the garden, which had a pool at the center and was surrounded on all four sides by a covered walkway. At the back of the garden was the door into the house. The first room was an atrium, which would have been used as a living room and a place to welcome visitors. It was open to the sky, allowing in light and fresh air. Bedrooms were located off the atrium. More rooms, including a dining room, were arranged around a courtyard at the back of the villa. In addition, there was a private bathhouse that could be reached from the garden walkway.

An artist's re-creation of the inside of an upper-class Roman home. At the front is the atrium, with curtained entryways leading to other rooms on each side.

Horace's country home was considered quite a modest place in comparison with those of many rich people. The walls of Pliny's seaside villa, for instance, enclosed more than forty rooms and outdoor areas. These included an atrium; bedrooms for himself, his slaves, and guests; four dining rooms, each looking out on a different view; storage rooms for grain and wine; a ball court; an exercise area; a sunroom; a study; two courtyards; an herb garden; a large garden with a covered walkway and a small vineyard; and "a terrace fragrant with violets," as Pliny wrote to a friend in a letter that proudly and lovingly described his seaside retreat. He was trying to persuade this friend to come visit him, so along with portraying the villa's beautiful setting, he made sure to mention his home's conveniences:

Young women exercising at a bathhouse

Next comes the broad and spacious cold room of the baths. It contains two bathing tubs which project outward, from opposite walls, with curved rims; they are quite large, especially considering how close the sea is. Nearby are the room for applying bath oil, the furnace room, a corridor, and then two small rooms. . . . Adjacent to these is a marvelous warm pool from which swimmers look out over the sea.

Wealthy Romans appreciated their comforts, and they loved to be surrounded by art, especially in their country homes. Walls would be deco-

⚘ HOW TO SET UP YOUR VILLA ❧

Columella, who was born in Spain, wrote his book *On Agriculture* during the first century. In this work, Columella gave plenty of advice on how to run a large estate. Here are some selections:

The size of a villa or housing structure should be determined by the total area of the farm; and the villa should be divided into three sections: one section resembling a city home [for the landowner], one section like a real farmhouse [for the workers and livestock], and the third section for storing farm products. . . .

A household slave

Now in the farmhouse part of the villa there should be a large kitchen with a high ceiling . . . so that the wood beams may be secure against the danger of fire. . . . The best plan will be to construct the cells for unchained slaves facing south. For those in chains let there be an underground prison, as healthful as possible. . . . For livestock there should be, within the villa, stalls which are not subject to either cold or heat. For draft and pack animals there should be two sets of stalls, winter ones and summer ones. . . . Cells for oxherds and shepherds should be placed next to their animals so that running out to care for them may be convenient. . . .

The third part of the villa, that designated for storing produce, is divided into rooms for oil, for oil and wine presses, for aged wine, and for wine not yet fermented; into lofts for hay and straw; and into areas for warehouses and granaries. . . . the wine room is placed on the ground floor; but it should be far removed from the bathrooms, the oven, the manure pile, and other filthy areas giving off a foul stench. . . .

Now the following things ought to be near the villa: an oven and flour mill . . . ; at least two ponds, one for the use of geese and cattle, the other for soaking lupines, elms, twigs, branches, and other things which have been adapted to our needs. There should also be two manure pits, one to receive fresh dung and to keep it for a year, the other to provide old dung, ready to be carted off. . . .

It is also a good idea to enclose fruit trees and gardens with a fence and to plant them close to the villa, in a place to which all the manure seepage from the barnyard and the bathrooms can flow, as well as the watery dregs squeezed from the olives. For both vegetables and trees also thrive on fertilizers of this sort.

rated with richly colored frescoes—or paintings—of landscapes, mythological scenes, or decorative designs. The floors were ornamented with mosaics, pictures or patterns made from small squares of stone. Some mosaics were in black and white, while others were in many colors. The furniture was of the highest quality. When wealthy people ate, they reclined on cushioned dining couches—three set around a low table—often in their gardens. The gardens themselves were enhanced by statues, fountains, and shrubs trimmed into various shapes, such as animals, words, ships, and even hunting scenes.

The water supply for rich and poor country dwellers alike usually came from wells and nearby springs, streams, or rivers. The wealthy, of course, enjoyed luxuries that were not available to others—for example, the rich could cover their windows with sheets of transparent mica or, more rarely, glass. Some very prosperous people had an underfloor heating system called a hypocaust. Otherwise, they generally relied on charcoal braziers for extra heat in their many rooms. The charcoal smoldered smokily, and to feel the brazier's warmth a person had to be almost right next to it. In winter, therefore, the rich might be almost as cold as the poor. They also made do with the same limited sources of artificial light—although wealthy people had ornate lampstands and candelabrums and could afford to use more oil and candles than poor people could.

IV
WORKING
THE LAND

THE FARMER CLEAVES THE EARTH WITH SHARE AND CURVING PLOUGH.
THERE IS HIS YEARLY WORK: THAT MAKES FOOD
FOR HIS HOME AND LITTLE ONES,
FOR HIS CATTLE AND WELL-DESERVING OXEN.
—VIRGIL, *GEORGICS*

ealthy landowners generally worked in the city in business and government. Rural property was an investment for them, a major source of wealth, but they very rarely took part in the actual work of the countryside. Of course, there were always a few landowners like Horace, who came to feel that he could only do his real work (writing poetry) in the peace of his farm. The poet wrote that he even enjoyed "digging and heaving rocks" from time to time. The future emperor Marcus Aurelius, too, thought that country chores could occasionally be fun: "we worked hard at picking grapes till we were covered with sweat and shouting with merriment," he said in a letter to his tutor, written from one of his family's estates. By and large, though, rural work was for the poor and unprivileged.

opposite:
A peasant or farm slave gathers up olives that have fallen to the ground.

29

SLAVE LABOR

Much of the labor on farms was done by slaves. Estate owners might have a great many; freeholders and tenant farmers, too, often had some slaves to help them with their work. Slavery was a fact of Roman life, as it was in most ancient civilizations. When the empire made new conquests, large numbers of war captives were enslaved. Slaves were also bought and sold in markets, many of which were located in Asia Minor. Children born to slaves automatically became slaves themselves. Sometimes referred to as "home-grown" slaves, they made up a large portion of the empire's enslaved population.

Uniquely for their time, the Romans very often freed their slaves. Freed slaves became Roman citizens, and their children could advance in society and even, occasionally, hold political office. Most rural slaves, however, did not enjoy such good fortune. Slaves who were freed were typically from the eastern part of the empire and worked in their owner's household, where he or she got to know them personally. Enslaved farm laborers, unless they were "home-grown," were generally from barbarian areas, such as Britain and Germany. Such slaves were unlikely to have a knowledge of Latin or Greek, or of the culture of the Mediterranean world. Moreover, they seldom came into contact with their masters. For these reasons, slaves who labored on large estates were almost never freed.

Farm slaves worked extremely hard, and they could be severely punished for any kind of disobedience. On some estates, owners kept unruly slaves chained together; they worked the fields as chain gangs during the day, and at night were locked in a prison. Pliny, however, assured one of his friends, "I myself never use chained slaves, nor does anyone else in this area." And Columella recommended that a master should personally make sure his slaves had decent food, clothing, and living conditions; should talk and even joke around with them; should allow them to complain about cruel treatment and then take action against it; and should reward especially

Captured Berbers, natives of North Africa, glumly wait to be sold as slaves.

good workers. All the same, many rural slaves endured very inhumane conditions. An example is found in this description of the often-beaten laborers at a flour mill, written by the second-century North African author Apuleius:

> Their skin was striped all over with livid scourge-scars; their wealed backs were crusted rather than clothed with their patchwork rags; some had no more covering than a bit of dangled apron; and every shirt was so tattered that the body was visible through the rents. Their brows were branded; their heads were half-shaved; irons clanked on their feet; their faces were sallow and ugly; the smoky gloom of the reeking overheated room had bleared and dulled their smarting eyes; and . . . their faces were wanly smeared with the dirty flour.

THE YEAR'S PATTERN

The realities of slave labor were far from the mind of Virgil when he wrote this loving description of a farm's seasonal cycle:

> Without delay the year's yield burgeons out in fruit
> or in young creatures or in nodding heads of grain,
> loading the furrows with the crop, overflowing the bins.
> Comes winter: then the generous olive yields its juice;
> the pigs come home jolly with acorns; berries flourish.
> Autumn too brings forth its various harvests; and high
> upon the sunlit rocks the vintage ripens mellow.

Farm animals had to be fed and cared for year-round.

In fact, Virgil's poems about farming, the *Georgics,* never mention slavery at all. In his time and in the parts of Italy where he lived, small farms worked by free men were probably the norm. But although freeholders, tenant farmers, and sharecroppers did not suffer the cruelties of slavery, they still endured many hardships and long hours to raise their animals and produce their crops. There was always work to be done, whatever the weather and season.

Naturally the year's agricultural activities varied from place to place, depending on climate and environment. In Italy, the farming year began in March, when grape vines were pruned and wheat was sown. By May the grain plants were well established, and the furrows where they grew had to be weeded and hoed. This was also the month for shearing sheep and washing wool. And before the coming of summer's heat, conscientious farmers fertilized their fields and orchards with manure and compost.

June was the time for cutting grass to dry for hay, which farm animals would eat during the winter. In July farmers harvested barley and beans. In August the wheat was ripe, and it had to be harvested without delay, before the crop could be destroyed by birds, rodents, or storms. After harvesting, the grain had to be dried, then threshed to break the head of grain from the straw, then winnowed to finish cleaning the grain of seed coatings and other chaff. Threshing and winnowing could go on for months—these tasks were fitted in whenever there was a break from other farm chores.

September saw the ripening of various fruits, and preparations were made for the vintage, or grape harvest, which came in October. Some grapes were selected for eating fresh, but most were destined to be turned into wine. This was a lengthy process, which began with pressing the juice out of the grapes. They were placed on a raised floor in a press room, where barefooted workers trod on them. Grooves or channels in the floor allowed the juice to run out into containers. A mechanical press might be used to get the remaining juice out of the grape pulp. The grape juice then fermented in large jars, barrels, or vats, until the wine was ready. Some estates produced a tremendous amount

Pressing olives to make olive oil was hard work.

of wine—archaeologists estimate that on one three-hundred-acre estate in central Italy, more than 250,000 gallons were made a year.

In November, farmers planted winter wheat and barley. December was the month for fertilizing grape vines, planting beans, and cutting wood. Moreover, olives were now ripe and ready to pick. They had to be handled carefully. Varro explained, "Olives that can be reached from the ground or from ladders should be picked rather than shaken down, because fruit that has been struck loses flesh and yields less oil. . . . Those that are out of reach should be beaten down, but with a reed rather than a pole." Some olives were intended to be eaten, but most were pressed to make olive oil. Both the grape and olive harvests required many extra workers, so landowners or farm managers would hire local people or, in some parts of the empire, nomads to help out.

After all of this, farmers got a bit of a rest in January. They cut willow branches and reeds for basket making and other uses, repaired tools, and the like. Then in February it was time to start tending the grapevines and weed the grain fields, getting them ready for the next planting.

OTHER OCCUPATIONS

While most people in the countryside worked at farming, rural areas also had some craftspeople, such as carpenters and blacksmiths; service workers, such as innkeepers and bakers; and what we would call professionals, particularly doctors and veterinarians. These people might be part of the labor force on a large estate, or they might live in a village and be available to anyone in the surrounding area.

A great many herders, in some parts of the empire, lived apart from village and estate life for much of the year. In spring they drove huge flocks of sheep or goats, or herds of cattle, up into mountain pastures, and there they stayed until autumn. This was a hard, lonely, and even dangerous existence. The herders followed their animals over steep and difficult terrain and were outdoors all day in all kinds of weather, with only little huts for shelter. As Varro wrote, "The type of man selected for this work should be strong, swift, agile and supple of limb; men who, as well as following the flock, can also defend it against wild beasts and robbers; men able to lift loads on to the backs of pack-animals, to dash out ahead, and to hurl javelins . . ."

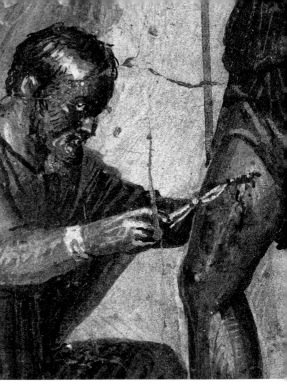

In coastal areas and around rivers and lakes, fishing was often more important than farming or herding. Some fishermen owned their own boats and equipment. Others might lease vessels and gear from someone else, in exchange for money or part of the catch. Seaside villas often included fish farms, with one or more tanks for breeding fish.

In this detail from a first-century fresco, a doctor concentrates on treating a man's injured leg.

Mining was the major activity in many rural districts. Most miners were slaves or convicts, and their lives were miserable. The historian Diodorus Siculus, toward the end of the first century B.C.E., wrote:

The slaves engaged in the operation of the mines . . . are physically destroyed, their bodies worn down from working in the mine shafts both day and night. Many die because of the excessive maltreatment they suffer. They are given no rest or break from their toil, but rather are forced by the whiplashes of the overseers to endure the most dreadful of hardships; thus do they wear out their lives in misery . . . although they often pray more for death than for life because of the magnitude of their suffering.

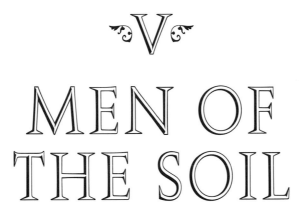

V

MEN OF THE SOIL

HAPPY IS THE MAN WHO REMAINS FAR FROM THE WORLD
OF BUSINESS, AS DID OUR PURITAN ANCESTORS,
AND WHO CULTIVATES THE FAMILY FARM WITH HIS OWN OXEN;
WHO REFRAINS FROM MONEYLENDING; WHO IS NOT A SOLDIER
ROUSED FROM SLEEP BY THE HARSH TRUMPET. . . .
—HORACE, *EPODES*

In a Roman family, the father was the absolute head of the household. He was responsible for taking care of the family property and making all financial decisions. It was his duty to work hard and provide for his wife, children, and slaves. They, in turn, were expected to treat him with great respect and to always behave in a way that would honor him. But from the first century B.C.E. on, writers frequently complained that these old virtues were being neglected in the cities. In the country, on the other hand, the traditional values were said to be alive and well. It is hard for us now to tell whether or not that common opinion was true, for farmers and farmworkers almost never wrote about themselves. We can assume, however, that they did carry on with such Roman virtues as tough-

opposite:
A portrait of a
Roman-Egyptian
man, his face
lined from care,
hard work, and
long hours in
the sun

ness, perseverance, and hard work—not as an ideal, but because these qualities were necessary for survival.

LEISURELY LANDOWNERS

Generation after generation of Romans learned the story of Cincinnatus, a role model of ideal manhood. In 458 B.C.E., he was out plowing his fields when members of the Roman Senate came to beg him to take command of the army. Cincinnatus did not hesitate to do his duty, and he led the army to a swift victory. Sixteen days later, he resigned his command and returned to his little cottage, his fields, and his plowing. Recalling the stories of Cincinnatus and other farmer-heroes, Columella wrote in the first century C.E.,

> I am reminded by the great number of written records that our ancestors regarded attention to farming as a matter of pride. . . . I realize that the manners and strenuous lifestyle of bygone days are out of favour with present-day extravagance. . . . all of us who are heads of families have abandoned the sickle and the plough, and slunk inside the city.

Of course, Columella was thinking only of upper-class heads of families. But one reason that he wrote his book on agriculture was to convince some of these men that "one way of increasing one's fortune that is upright and above board . . . comes from cultivating the soil." He wanted landowners, even if they didn't work their estates with their own hands, to at least have a thorough knowledge of the principles of agriculture and farm management. That way they could appoint the right kind of men as bailiffs and foremen, they could make sound decisions about land usage and the like, and

A model of Pliny's seaside villa, clearly a place to relax and enjoy the good life

their estates would be as productive—and profitable—as possible.

Pliny the Younger was one landowner who took his responsibilities quite seriously. In a letter to a friend, he declared, "I am totally involved in farming," referring to his financial investments. He went on to ask the friend's advice about whether or not he should buy a certain piece of property. On another occasion, Pliny wrote to the emperor Trajan requesting a thirty-day leave of absence from his government duties so that he could go out to the countryside to settle some problems on one of his estates.

Several of Pliny's letters described not the responsibilities, but the pleasures of owning country property. He wrote of the leisure time he enjoyed when visiting his various villas. He slept as late as he wanted in the morning and lay about for a while thinking and then dictating letters or literary works to his secretary. A few hours later he went out and sat on the terrace to meditate and dictate some more. Then it was time for a carriage or horseback ride, followed by a nap. After that he might read aloud from a Greek or Latin speech. This would be followed by a walk, some exercise, and a bath. While he ate dinner with his wife and a few others, a slave often read a book to them. Then everyone would enjoy some music

ᴥ A FREEHOLDER'S LIFE: ᴧ
DAYDREAM VS. REALITY

Upper-class men were expected to lead useful lives serving the public, participating in politics and government, or managing vast business interests. So perhaps it is no wonder that upper-class poets often portrayed country life as an escape from reality. "Let another man heap up for himself the wealth of shining gold," wrote Tibullus. "May I be content to live on a little, . . . to avoid the summer's heat under the shade of a tree upon the bank of a flowing stream. And let me not think it shameful to hold a hoe once in a while."

This vision of a life of rural leisure contrasts sharply with an anonymous poet's realistic portrayal of a small freeholder's morning:

ᴥᴥᴧ

Simulus, the peasant farmer of a meager little plot, worried about gnawing hunger on this coming day. He slowly raised his weary limbs from his ugly little cot. With anxious hand he groped through the stagnant darkness and felt his way to the fireplace, burning his hand when he touched it. . . . With frequent huffs and puffs, he stirred up the sluggish fire. . . .

He unlocked the cupboard door with a key. Spread out on the cupboard floor was a paltry pile of grain. From this he took for himself as much as his measuring bucket held. He moved over to the mill and put his trusty lamp on a small shelf. . . . Then he slipped off his outer garment and, clad only in a shaggy goatskin, he swept the stones and inner portion of the mill. He put both his hands to work. . . . The grain which was ground by the rapid blows of the millstone poured out as flour. . . . At times he sang country songs and eased his labor with a rural tune. Or he shouted for Scybale. She was his only companion, an African woman. . . . He called her and told her to put firewood on the fireplace and to heat up some cold water. . . . [He mixed the flour with water and salt, formed a round loaf of bread, and put it to bake over the hearthfire. Then] hard-working Scybale plucked the bread out of the fireplace. Simulus happily took a piece in his hand. Now that he had put aside the fear of hunger and was free of anxiety, at least for this day, he tied leggings on his legs, covered his head with a leather cap, yoked his obedient oxen, drove them into the field, and sank his plow into the earth.

or a dramatic reading of a comedy. Before bed, Pliny took one more walk, along with some of his better-educated slaves, enjoying their conversation. This, he wrote, was his favorite routine, but sometimes it varied. He might join a hunting party (although he took writing materials with him, and usually worked on something literary while others pursued the quarry), or friends might drop by for a visit. And, of course, now and then he had to devote his attention to his tenant farmers and their complaints.

TENANT FARMERS

In one of his letters, Pliny told a friend that on some of his lands the tenants had gotten so far behind in paying their rents, they would never be able to catch up. Pliny decided that the best solution to this problem would be "to let out the farms on a share-cropping basis instead of a money rent, and then make some of my servants overseers to keep a watch on the harvest." These tenants were lucky that Pliny was willing to try a new arrangement with them. In many cases, when a tenant got behind in paying his rent, the landowner would seize and sell his equipment, slaves, livestock, and seed grain. This brought the tenant up-to-date on his rent in the short term—but he no longer had the resources to farm his holding.

Tenants on private estates typically leased their land for five years at a time. A wise landowner generally preferred to rent a holding to the same tenant over and over; the tenant would tend to think of the land almost as his own, and so would take better care of it. When he died, the lease might even pass to his son. The emperors came to encourage a similar stability on their estates. From the reign of Hadrian in the first part of the second century, an imperial tenant who brought new land into cultivation was guaranteed this land for the rest of his life. If he planted a fig orchard or vineyard, he could even have the land rent-free for five years; planting an olive orchard earned him ten years without rent.

Unlike wealthy landowners, tenant farmers and sharecroppers had very few opportunities for leisure. There were holidays, of course, when they did not work. Sometimes bad weather would give them a break from the heaviest outdoor chores. Then they might spend their time making baskets or nets, or mending tools. While engaged in such activities, they could also enjoy conversation and storytelling with family and friends. Now and then, a farmer might get away from his fields for a bit to go hunting or fishing. These could be relaxing activities, and if he was successful he would also have fresh meat or fish to bring home to his family. According to Virgil, who was probably thinking about the farmers of northern Italy, wintertime in particular brought opportunities for relaxation, enjoying company, and hunting:

> Winter's the tenant's rest.
> In the cold weather farmers mostly enjoy their gains,
> happily occupied in giving mutual parties.
> The genial winter's invitation frees from care. . . .
> But even so then is the time to gather acorns
> and bay-berries and olives and the blood-red myrtle;
> time to set snares for game-birds and nets for the stag
> and to pursue the long-eared hare; time to shoot deer,
> whirling the hempen thongs of a Balearic sling,
> when snow lies deep, when rivers hustle ice along.

·VI·
RURAL WOMEN

DELIA WILL GUARD THE HARVEST
IN HOT SUNSHINE UPON THE THRESHING-FLOOR;
OR SHE WILL SUPERVISE THE GRAPES HEAPING THE WINE-VATS
AND WATCH THE WHITE MUST* TRODDEN BY NIMBLE FEET. . . .
LET HER DIRECT THE WORK, AND GOVERN ALL THE WORKERS.
—TIBULLUS, *Elegies*

nder Roman law, free women did not enjoy the same status as free men. A woman nearly always had a male guardian—her father, husband, or another relative. In the case of a freedwoman, her guardian was generally her former master. The guardian was supposed to advise the woman on all her legal and financial dealings. Some guardians, however, gave their wards considerable freedom to make their own decisions. And a freeborn woman who bore three children was released from guardianship; four children earned a freedwoman the same privilege.

With or without guardians, though, women were still allowed to buy, sell, own, and inherit land. Pliny's letters give us two examples: in one, he offered to sell some of his lakefront property in northern

*grape pulp and skins

opposite:
Mosaic portrait of a young woman from southeastern Asia Minor

Italy to a woman friend. In another, he wrote to the manager of the farm that he had given to his old nurse, urging him to make the farm as profitable as possible so that the nurse would have a good living. Another example comes from a town in what is now Tunisia, where one of the area's major landowners in the second century was a woman named Valeria Atticilla. We also know that women owned luxurious seaside villas on the Bay of Naples, south of Rome.

WIVES AND MOTHERS

In Roman culture, a woman's main tasks in life were to marry, to care for her husband and his home, and to bear children to be his heirs. Fulfilling these roles, she was expected to uphold such traditional virtues as modesty, respectability, faithfulness, conscientiousness, and thriftiness.

Although many babies in wealthy families were fed by wet nurses, most Roman women nursed their own children.

These ideals originated in Rome, and they spread to the upper classes throughout the empire. People living in rural communities in many provinces, however, often kept more to their own traditions. In some places, therefore, women had more rights and status than in Italy, but in other places they had fewer.

Girls married as young as eleven or twelve; by the age of thirty, a woman might well be a grandmother. A great many women, however, did not live that long. Childbirth was very difficult and dangerous in the ancient world. There were few medical techniques that could help a woman if something went wrong, and both mother and baby might well die. This tombstone inscription from what is now Hungary tells a common story:

> Here I lie, a matron named Veturia. . . . I lived for twenty-seven years, and I was married for sixteen years to the same man. After I gave birth to six children, only one of whom is still alive, I died. Titus Julius Fortunatus, a soldier of Legion II Adiutrix, provided this memorial for his wife, who was incomparable and showed outstanding devotion to him.

In memorials like this one, a husband often expressed his feelings for his dead wife, praising her virtues and the harmony of their marriage. Sometimes wives set up similar memorials for their husbands. Judging from these inscriptions and other sources, the ideal marriage was one where the couple lived together in peace, contentment, and mutual respect. Romantic love was perhaps not as important—since most marriages were arranged, the couple might not even know each other very well before their wedding. But often love grew. Once when Pliny's wife Calpurnia was staying in the countryside to recover from an illness, Pliny wrote to her from Rome, "It is incred-

A family portrait from an Italian villa

ible how much I miss you, because I love you and then because we are not used to being separated. And so I lie awake most of the night haunted by your image; and during the day, . . . my feet lead me, they really do, to your room; and then I turn and leave, sick at heart and sad."

HARD WORKERS

An upper-class woman did very little work other than supervising her slaves. Traditionally, though, women of every class spent much of their time spinning, weaving, and sewing. This was true of nearly all women in the countryside, as Tibullus poetically expressed it:

> The handiwork of dainty girls comes from the country—
>   the soft fleece grown by a pure white sheep:
> that is the work of women too, who turn the distaff
>   and whirl the spindle round with agile thumbs;
> meanwhile some busy indefatigable* weaver
>   sings, as the swinging loom-weights clash and ring.

Like rural women in most times and places, tenant farmers' wives probably did many farm chores. The bulk of their activity, though, likely involved preserving and preparing food, along with making cloth and clothing. Women slaves in the countryside did a variety of work, caring for farm animals and laboring in the fields, but Columella recommended that on cold or rainy days they instead do wool work. For slaves this would include cleaning and carding the wool as well as spinning it into thread.

Some female slaves accompanied shepherds up to the mountain pastures. These women, Varro explained, "can follow the flocks,

*tireless

48

prepare the shepherds' meals, and make the men more attentive to their work." He added that when he visited what is now Bosnia, he observed that the women there "are as good workers as the men . . . they can either do the shepherding, or bring logs for the fire and cook the food, or look after the farm implements [tools] in the huts."

The most important female slave on a large estate was the forewoman, who was the foreman's companion and assistant. (Usually they had a relationship like husband and wife, but slaves were not allowed to be legally married.) The forewoman's duties were wide-ranging. This selection from Columella's book covers just a portion of them:

While watching over her flock, a shepherdess also spins woolen thread using a distaff (in her left hand) and drop spindle.

> At one moment she will have to go to the loom and teach the weavers whatever she knows better than them. . . . At another moment, she will have to check on those slaves who are preparing the food for the *familia* [household]. Then she will also have to see that the kitchen, cowsheds, and even the stables are cleaned. And she will also have to open up the sick-rooms occasionally, even if they are empty of patients, and keep them free of dirt. . . . She will, in addition, have to be in attendance when the stewards of the pantry and cellar are weighing something, and also be present when the shepherds are milking in the stables. . . . But she will also certainly

～ BARBARIAN WOMEN ～

In some areas that the Romans conquered, women had a higher status than in the Mediterranean world. In fact, among the people whom Greeks and Romans referred to as barbarians, women could hold positions of great influence, even becoming political and religious leaders. Tacitus wrote that German warriors valued the praise of the women of their families more than any other praise. When injured, men went to their mothers and wives to have their wounds healed. According to tradition, sometimes when men were near to losing a battle, women's constant urging gave them the inspira-

The British queen Boudicca, as imagined by a nineteenth-century artist

tion and strength to win victory after all. "Moreover," Tacitus wrote, "they believe that within women there is a certain holiness and spirit of prophecy, and so the men do not scorn to ask their advice, nor do they ignore the women's answers."

The most famous British leader of Roman times was Boudicca, queen of the Iceni tribe in eastern Britain. In 61 C.E. she led a rebellion that nearly succeeded in driving the Romans out of Britain entirely. The historian Dio Cassius imagined her urging her warriors with words that voiced the anger many ruled by Rome must have felt:

> You have learned by actual experience how different freedom is from slavery. Hence, even if anyone of you had previously . . . been deceived by the alluring promises of the Romans, . . . you have learned how great a mistake you made in preferring an imported despotism to your ancestral mode of life. . . . For what treatment is there of the most shameful or grievous sort that we have not suffered since these men made their appearance in Britain? Have we not been robbed entirely of our greatest possessions, while for those that remain we pay taxes? Besides pasturing and tilling for them . . . do we not pay a yearly tribute for our very bodies? . . . We have . . . been despised and trampled underfoot by men who know nothing else than how to secure gain.

need to be present when the sheep are sheared, and to examine the wool carefully.

A rural slave woman's other major duty was to give birth to children, who would be the property of the master—"home-grown" slaves were generally considered to be the best workers. Columella wrote that he rewarded slave women who bore several children. A woman who had three children was exempted from work (other than caring for the children, we assume). If she had four or more, she was given her freedom. The children, however, remained slaves.

·VII·
GROWING UP IN THE COUNTRYSIDE

FATHERS ORDER THEIR CHILDREN TO BE WOKEN UP TO DO THEIR
WORK EARLY. EVEN ON HOLIDAYS THEY DON'T ALLOW THEM TO BE
IDLE, AND THEY WRING SWEAT AND SOMETIMES TEARS FROM THEM.
BUT MOTHERS WANT TO HOLD THEIR CHILDREN ON THEIR LAPS AND
KEEP THEM IN THE COOL SHADE; THEY WANT THEM NEVER TO BE
MADE UNHAPPY, NEVER TO WEEP, AND NEVER TO BE IN DISTRESS.
—SENECA THE YOUNGER, *AN ESSAY ABOUT PROVIDENCE*

L ike everything else in the Roman Empire, childhood experiences depended on many factors: whether you were rich or poor, free or slave, sickly or healthy; whether you lived in the country or the city; whether you were in the provinces or in Italy. Your mother might not live through childbirth, or she might die from complications during another pregnancy. Your father might be a good deal older than your mother and die while you are still a child. Or your parents could get divorced, in which case you would stay with your father. If your widowed or divorced parent remarried—

opposite:
A beautiful marble statue of a child hugging a young swan

which was common—then you would have a stepparent and probably stepbrothers and stepsisters. On top of everything else, you would be very fortunate simply to live through childhood: scholars estimate that 44 percent of Roman children died before their tenth birthday.

COMING INTO THE WORLD

In the Roman Empire, nearly all babies were born at home. In the countryside, however, some hardworking women had their babies outdoors. Varro related that when he was traveling in what is now Bosnia, he saw that "pregnant women, when the time for delivery has arrived, often withdraw a short distance from where they are working, give birth there, and come back with the child you would think they had found, not borne." Afterward these women carried their babies around with them while they worked; Varro saw women nursing their babies even while they were hauling firewood.

Some babies, unfortunately, did not receive a joyful welcome.

Little babies, like this newborn being handed to its mother, were wrapped in swaddling clothes to keep them feeling warm and secure.

Because there was no reliable method of family planning, parents might already have more children than they could provide for. An extra mouth to feed could be a real burden. There were very few public assistance programs for families in this position, especially in the countryside; nor were there foster-care systems or adoption agencies. Some impoverished parents felt their only option was to expose, or abandon, their newborns, leaving them outdoors to either die or be picked up by a passerby.

This was a common practice throughout the ancient world.

It was the father's decision whether to raise a baby or expose it. Men were more likely to abandon daughters than sons, because it was felt that girls could not contribute as much to the family, and they would require dowries in order to get married. A mythological story retold by Ovid in his *Metamorphoses* was based on such a situation:

> Ligdus . . . was a poor man. . . . He told his pregnant wife . . . , "I pray for two things—that you may have an easy labor, and that you may bear a male child. For a daughter is too burdensome, and we just don't have the money. . . . I say this with great reluctance, so please forgive me—if you should bear a girl, we'll have to kill her."
>
> He spoke the words, and they both wept. . . . And Telethusa begged her husband over and over again to change his mind, but in vain. . . .
>
> She went into labor and gave birth to a girl. But the father didn't know this. And the mother lied, and raised her daughter as a boy.

A BRIEF CHILDHOOD

Upper-class children were largely cared for by slaves, often including a woman who nursed them. But most rural babies were breastfed by their own mothers, probably for about two years. A peasant mother had little assistance with childcare, unless she had an older daughter who could help out.

Soon after children were toddling, they were probably given simple chores to do. Still, while they were quite young, they did have some playtime. Most rural children were likely to have few toys. On

A group of young girls at play

the other hand, they would find plenty of things around the farmyard and fields to play with. A fallen branch could be a pretend sword; a large flower might make a beautiful, if not long-lasting, doll. A poem by Tibullus mentions country children building miniature cottages out of sticks. There was also plenty of room to run around in the fresh air, and we know that children enjoyed games similar to leapfrog, tag, and blindman's buff.

Various ball games were popular, too, including ones that resembled dodgeball, soccer, and field hockey. On a farm it was easy to find materials to make a ball. Some ancient types of balls were made of wool. Others were constructed from inflated pig bladders wrapped tightly in pigskin or leather. A ball that bounced fairly well could be made from cut-up sponges with string wound around them to make a sphere, all sewn into a cloth cover.

Young people then, as now, were often high-spirited. And if they happened to be rich kids on a visit to their country estates, they sometimes were not very considerate of the hardworking locals. Young men might be particularly rowdy and likely to disrupt peasants' routines. In the following passage, Marcus Aurelius—heir to the imperial throne and future philosopher—gleefully writes to his tutor about the trouble he caused for two shepherds and their flock:

When father was on the way home from the vineyards I jumped on my horse as I always do and set off down the road.

I hadn't gone far when I saw a large flock of sheep huddled together in the road as they do in places where the way is narrow. There were four dogs and two shepherds and nothing else. Then one of the shepherds, when he spotted our little gang riding up, shouted to the other one, "See them horsemen? They're the biggest robbers out!" When I heard this I dug my spurs into my horse and galloped straight into the sheep. They scattered in panic . . . baa-ing and bleating. One of the shepherds hurled his crook and it struck the man riding behind me. We beat it! The shepherd who was worried about losing his sheep broke his crook!

The older a child got, the more work he or she was expected to do, whether slave or free. Girls were taught wool working quite young. On estates, slave girls and boys looked after the sheep and goats that were kept on the farm. (Only grown men and women went with the flocks to distant pastures.) By the time they were ten or eleven, most rural children were working just as hard as the adults, and at almost as many tasks. The only things they really couldn't do yet were the jobs that took a lot of strength, such as plowing. But before many more years passed, they would be getting married and taking their full places in the adult world.

Nearly half of all Roman children died before they were ten years old. A grieving family had this statue placed on the lid of their child's sarcophagus, or stone coffin.

GROWING UP IN THE COUNTRYSIDE

·VIII·

HARD TIMES AND HOLIDAYS

DRIVE DISEASES FAR AWAY. MAY MEN AND BEASTS BE HEALTHY. . . .
MAY I DRIVE HOME MY FLOCK AS NUMEROUS AS THEY WERE
AT DAYBREAK. . . . LET DIRE HUNGER NOT COME MY WAY.
LET THERE BE ABUNDANCE OF GRAIN. . . .
—OVID, *CALENDAR*

 e have seen that everyday life could be full of hardships for most country dwellers. Diseases, of both people and animals, added to the burdens. Many illnesses and injuries that can easily be treated now, or even prevented in the first place, were fatal in the ancient world. There were not as many medicines available, and there was a less thorough knowledge of the workings of the human body and of surgical techniques. The possibility of crop failure also made famine a constant danger, and malnutrition was common.

A drought or other calamity could become even worse because of greed. For instance, in the late second century Galen, a doctor, wrote about what happened in one area that had suffered several years of bad harvests. The people of the town went out and "took from the

opposite:
Special events could give people of the Roman Empire a break from the hard work of their daily lives. These men are waiting at the finish line to honor the winner of a chariot race.

fields all the wheat, with the barley, beans and lentils." Because of this, the country dwellers had nothing to eat except "twigs and shoots of trees, bulbs and roots of unwholesome plants, and . . . wild vegetables." Nearly all the rural people developed diseases related to malnutrition, as well as conditions such as ulcers and tumors.

WAR AND PEACE

There was one hardship that most people in the Roman Empire were safe from during the first two centuries C.E. That was warfare, which in other times and places throughout history has taken a terrible toll on the countryside and its inhabitants. There were, of course, people who resented Roman rule and the military occupation of their lands, and sometimes these resentments flared up into rebellions. But most of the empire's residents seemed to agree with Tacitus when he wrote, "if the Romans are driven out—which Heaven forbid!—what will follow except universal war among all peoples?"

Thanks to Rome's strength, only communities near the empire's borders really had to worry about being attacked. This is the situation described by Ovid, living in exile on the west coast of the Black Sea, less than a hundred miles from the Danube frontier:

> Countless tribes round about threaten cruel war, thinking it base to live if not by plunder. . . . When least expected, the foe swarms upon us like birds, and when scarce well seen is already driving off the booty. . . . Rare then is he who ventures to till the fields, for the wretch must plow with one hand, and hold arms in the other. The shepherd wears a helmet . . . and instead of a wolf the timorous ewes dread war.

CELEBRATING THE SEASONS

The weekend was unknown in the Roman Empire, although its Jewish population did observe a weekly day of rest. For others, every day was a workday—unless it was a holiday. Fortunately, there were many of these. On some of them, most work was forbidden by law—but farmers might feel that they had too much to do and could not afford to rest. Virgil wrote:

> Yes, even on holy days laws human and divine
> permit some work to be done. No ordinance forbids
> to irrigate the sown field or to fence it off,
> make ready snares for birds, burn up briers and thorns.

Slaves also had to work when others were relaxing and celebrating, although we know that some slaves, at least, were guaranteed a certain number of days off a year. When farmers did get to rest and enjoy a holiday, they liked to gather together family and friends—and often the laborers, too—for eating, drinking, and dancing. Country celebrations were usually outdoors, and in the summer people might build leafy bowers to provide extra shade. There might also be competitions, such as footraces, wrestling matches, and javelin-throwing contests. Nearly all Roman holidays had a religious significance, so prayers and ceremonies played a part in the day's activities, too.

Music and dance enlivened many celebrations. The man here is playing a double flute, while the woman not only dances but also plays castanet-like instruments.

A number of Roman festivals honored the events of the agricultural year. Naturally, these were particularly beloved celebrations in the countryside. Some of the most important were the Terminalia, the Parilia, the Robigalia, and the Ambarvalia.

The Terminalia occurred on February 23, when neighbors gathered at their *terminus,* the stone or post that marked the boundary between their lands. The head of each family placed on the *terminus* a small cake and a garland of flowers, and they set up an altar in front of it. Then, in the words of Ovid,

> Hither the farmer's country wife brings with her own hands on a sherd the fire which she has taken from her own warm hearth. The old man chops up wood. . . . Then he gets the kindling flames going with dry bark; his boy stands by holding the broad basket. After he has tossed corn [grain] three times into the fire his little daughter offers the pieces of honeycomb. Others hold out jars of wine; portions of each are cast into the flames. The company, dressed in white, look on in holy silence.

The Parilia arrived on April 21. This festival honored Pales, the goddess of shepherds. In the morning, shepherds or flock owners faced the east and repeated a prayer four times, asking the goddess to protect both people and animals. At the end of the prayers, the worshipper washed with the morning dew, then made an offering of mixed milk and wine. At the celebration's peak, sheep were driven through the smoke of a bonfire to purify them. Then, as the flames died down, shepherds took turns leaping over the fire.

On April 25 came the Robigalia, which often took place in a

grove of trees. This holiday's ceremonies were designed to keep rust and mildew away from the ripening grain. Ovid recorded a prayer to the god of rust, which included this appeal: "Put your hands on hard iron, not on tender crops. First destroy objects which can destroy others. . . . Let the hoes and the mattock and the curved plowshare, let all the farm equipment shine brightly, but let rust blemish weapons of war."

The Ambarvalia, at the end of May, was a day of purifying the fields and crops. No one was supposed to do any work, including the oxen who usually pulled the plow—they were left in their stalls, garlanded with flowers and given extra hay to eat. Everyone who wanted to take part in the ceremony was required to put on clean clothes and wash their hands in running water. Then they made a silent procession around the boundaries of the fields, leading a pig, a sheep, and a bull. Later there would be a feast, with music, singing, and dancing into the night.

Life in the Roman Empire was hard, full of suffering for many and never-ending work for most. Yet there was much beauty, too, as poets and painters have shown us in their images of the countryside. Those who lived close to the land paid attention to its natural cycles and honored them with prayers and celebrations. The humblest farmer knew that a spring of pure water or a grove of trees was something special. The ancient Romans can inspire us, too, to take time now and then to remember the preciousness of nature and our rural areas, and to think gratefully of the many people who work so hard on farms around the world.

The Romans developed early versions of many of our modern musical instruments. These men are playing a small organ and the ancestor of the French horn.

GLOSSARY

atrium the front room of a Roman house, used to receive visitors

bailiff a landowner's agent, who managed all or part of his property for him

barbarian a person whose language could not be understood. For the Romans, barbarians were people and nations who did not speak Latin or Greek and did not share in Greco-Roman culture—and because of this, they were often felt to be uncivilized and somewhat inferior.

brazier a pan to hold smoldering charcoal, usually supported by a tripod or other stand, used as a heat source

dowry money, goods, and/or property that a bride's family gave her to bring into her marriage

freeholders people who owned and farmed their own land; sometimes called smallholders, since such farms were usually just large enough to support a family

fresco a wall painting made on fresh plaster

inscription words written on or carved into lasting materials such as metal and stone

javelin a type of spear

legion a unit of the Roman army, made up of about five thousand men

matron a freeborn married woman

mattock a digging tool similar to a pickax

mosaic a picture or design made from small square stones. In cheaper mosaics, the stones might be painted or dyed; the best mosaics used stones in a wide range of natural colors.

procurator an official who ran an estate or mine on behalf of the emperor

province a territory of the Roman Empire

sharecropper a farmer who worked land owned by someone else. Instead of paying rent for his farm, a sharecropper gave the landowner a portion of whatever he raised.

tenant farmer a farmer who rented his farm from a landowner

tribute the taxes—in particular grain and other products—that a province had to pay to the Roman government

villa a country home or estate

wattle and daub a building technique using a framework of wooden posts with flexible sticks woven between them (the wattle), filled in with a mixture of mud, clay, and straw (the daub)

FOR FURTHER READING

Amery, Heather, and Patricia Vanags. *Rome & Romans.* London: Usborne, 1997.

Corbishley, Mike. *What Do We Know about the Romans?* New York: Peter Bedrick Books, 1991.

Dargie, Richard. *A Roman Villa.* Austin, TX, and New York: Raintree Steck-Vaughn, 2000.

Denti, Mario. *Journey to the Past: Imperial Rome.* Austin, TX, and New York: Raintree Steck-Vaughn, 2001.

Ganeri, Anita. *How Would You Survive as an Ancient Roman?* New York: Franklin Watts, 1995.

Hart, Avery, and Sandra Gallagher. *Ancient Rome! Exploring the Culture, People and Ideas of This Powerful Empire.* Charlotte, VT: Williamson Publishing, 2002.

Hinds, Kathryn. *The Ancient Romans.* New York: Benchmark Books, 1997.

Jovinelly, Joann, and Jason Netelkos. *The Crafts and Culture of the Romans.* New York: Rosen Publishing Group, 2002.

Macdonald, Fiona. *Women in Ancient Rome.* New York: Peter Bedrick Books, 2000.

Morley, Jacqueline. *A Roman Villa: Inside Story.* New York: Peter Bedrick Books, 1992.

Nardo, Don. *Life in Ancient Rome.* San Diego: Lucent Books, 1997.

———. *Life of a Roman Soldier.* San Diego: Lucent Books, 2001.

———. *The Roman Empire.* San Diego: Lucent Books, 1994.

ONLINE INFORMATION*

Carr, Karen E. *History for Kids: Ancient Rome.*
    http://www.historyforkids.org/learn/romans/index.htm

Frischer, Bernard. *The Website of the Horace's Villa Project.*
    http://www.humnet.ucla.edu/horaces-villa
Goldberg, Dr. Neil. *The Rome Project.*
    http://www.dalton.org/groups/rome/index.html
Knight International. *Camelot Village: Britain's Heritage and History: Roman Farms.*
    http://www.camelotintl.com/romans/farming.html
Kowalski, Wladyslaw Jan. *Roman Ball Games.*
    http://www.personal.psu.edu/users/w/x/wxk116/romeball.html
Michael C. Carlos Museum of Emory University. *Odyssey Online: Rome.*
    http://carlos.emory.edu/ODYSSEY/ROME/homepg.html
Nova Online. *Secrets of Lost Empires: Roman Bath.*
    http://www.pbs.org/wgbh/nova/lostempires/roman
Roman Open Air Museum.
    http://www.villa-rustica.de/intro/indexe.html
Warrior Challenge: Romans.
    http://www.pbs.org/wnet/warriorchallenge/romans/

*All Internet sites were available and accurate when this book was sent to press.

BIBLIOGRAPHY

Adkins, Lesley, and Roy A. Adkins. *Handbook to Life in Ancient Rome.* New York and Oxford: Oxford University Press, 1994.

Apuleius. *The Golden Ass.* Translated by Jack Lindsay. Bloomington: Indiana University Press, 1962.

Boardman, John, et al., eds. *The Oxford Illustrated History of the Roman World.* Oxford and New York: Oxford University Press, 1988.

Cornell, Tim, and John Matthews. *The Roman World.* Alexandria, VA: Stonehenge Press, 1991.

Editors of Time-Life Books. *Rome: Echoes of Imperial Glory.* Alexandria, VA: Time-Life Books, 1994.

Editors of Time-Life Books. *What Life Was Like when Rome Ruled the World: The Roman Empire 100 BC–AD 200.* Alexandria, VA: Time-Life Books, 1997.

Fantham, Elaine, et al. *Women in the Classical World: Image and Text.* New York and Oxford: Oxford University Press, 1994.

Grant, Michael. *The World of Rome.* New York: Praeger Publications, 1969.

Hallett, Judith P. "Women in the Ancient Roman World." In *Women's Roles in Ancient Civilizations: A Reference Guide,* edited by Bella Vivante, 257–289. Westport, CT: Greenwood Press, 1999.

Highet, Gilbert. *Poets in a Landscape.* New York: Alfred A. Knopf, 1957.

James, Peter, and Nick Thorpe. *Ancient Inventions.* New York: Ballantine Books, 1994.

Lewis, Naphtali, and Meyer Reinhold, eds. *Roman Civilization, Sourcebook II: The Empire.* New York: Harper & Row, 1966.

Shelton, Jo-Ann. *As the Romans Did: A Source Book in Roman Social History.* 2nd ed. New York and Oxford: Oxford University Press, 1998.

Tacitus. *Dialogus, Agricola, Germania.* Latin text, with facing-page translation by Sir William Peterson. Cambridge, MA: Harvard University Press, 1914.

Vitruvius. *The Ten Books on Architecture.* Translated by Morris Hicky Morgan. New York: Dover Publications, 1960.

Wells, Colin. *The Roman Empire.* 2nd ed. Cambridge, MA: Harvard University Press, 1992.

White, K. D. *Country Life in Classical Times.* Ithaca, NY: Cornell University Press, 1977.

SOURCES FOR QUOTATIONS

Chapter I

p. 1 "Then let me love": Highet, *Poets in a Landscape,* p. 57.

p. 2 "through this, Rome became": ibid., p. 59.

p. 2 "Those were the sons": ibid., p. 129.

p. 3 "Happy—even too happy": ibid., p. 57.

p. 4 "From the day": White, *Country Life in Classical Times,* p. 93.

p. 6 "Do you ask": ibid., p. 49.

p. 8 "Up until this day": Shelton, *As the Romans Did,* pp. 286–287.

Chapter II

p. 11 "Hail, earthly paradise": Highet, *Poets in a Landscape,* p. 62.

p. 12 "Often the farmer": White, *Country Life in Classical Times,* p. 10.

p. 13 "It is well known": Tacitus, *Dialogus, Agricola, Germania,* pp. 287 and 301.

p. 14 "Anyone living": Wells, *The Roman Empire,* pp. 227–228.

p. 15 "I always leave": Highet, *Poets in a Landscape,* p. 136.

Chapter III

p. 19 "If we must live": Highet, *Poets in a Landscape,* p. 153.

p. 19 "With [animal] skins": Lewis, *Roman Civilization,* p. 107.

p. 20 "On the other hand": Vitruvius, *The Ten Books on Architecture,* pp. 39–40.

p. 22 "So, when the gods": White, *Country Life in Classical Times,* pp. 47–48.

p. 24 "In a poor cottage": Highet, *Poets in a Landscape,* p. 153.

p. 25 "a terrace": Shelton, *As the Romans Did,* p. 77.

p. 25 "Next comes the broad": ibid., p. 77.

p. 26 "The size of a villa": ibid., pp. 72–74.

Chapter IV

p. 29 "The farmer cleaves": Highet, *Poets in a Landscape,* p. 58.

p. 29 "digging and heaving rocks": ibid., p. 137.

p. 29 "we worked hard": White, *Country Life in Classical Times,* p. 73.

p. 30 "I myself never": Shelton, *As the Romans Did,* p. 146.

p. 31 "Their skin was striped": Apuleius, *The Golden Ass,* p. 192.

p. 32 "Without delay the year's": Highet, *Poets in a Landscape,* p. 58.

p. 34 "Olives that can": White, *Country Life in Classical Times,* p. 71.

p. 35 "The type of man": ibid., p. 75.

p. 35 "The slaves engaged": Shelton, *As the Romans Did,* p. 172.

Chapter V

p. 37 "Happy is the man": Shelton, *As the Romans Did,* p. 161.

p. 38 "I am reminded": White, *Country Life in Classical Times,* p. 20.

p. 38 "one way of increasing": ibid., p. 19.

p. 39 "I am totally involved": Boardman, *The Oxford Illustrated History of the Roman World,* p. 353.

p. 40 "Let another man": Shelton, *As the Romans Did,* p. 161.

p. 40 "Simulus, the peasant farmer": ibid., pp. 157–158.

p. 42 "to let out": White, *Country Life in Classical Times,* p. 92.

p. 43 "Winter's the tenant's": ibid., p. 61.

Chapter VI

p. 45 "Delia will guard": Highet, *Poets in a Landscape,* p. 163.

p. 47 "Here I lie": Shelton, *As the Romans Did,* p. 290.

p. 47 "It is incredible": ibid., p. 46.

p. 48 "The handiwork": Highet, *Poets in a Landscape,* p. 168.

pp. 48, 49 "can follow" and "are as good": White, *Country Life in Classical Times,* pp. 75–76.

p. 49 "At one moment": Shelton, *As the Romans Did,* p. 305.

p. 50 "Moreover, they believe": Tacitus, *Dialogus, Agricola, Germania;* author's translation of Latin text, pp. 274, 276.

p. 50 "You have learned": Lewis, *Roman Civilization,* p. 415.

Chapter VII

p. 53 "Fathers order": Shelton, *As the Romans Did,* p. 22.

p. 54 "pregnant women": White, *Country Life in Classical Times,* p. 76.

p. 55 "Ligdus . . . was a poor man": Shelton, *As the Romans Did,* pp. 28–29.

p. 56 "When father was": White, *Country Life in Classical Times,* p. 83.

Chapter VIII

p. 59 "Drive diseases": White, *Country Life in Classical Times,* p. 102.

p. 59 "took from the fields" and "twigs and shoots": Wells, *The Roman Empire,* p. 246.

p. 60 "if the Romans": Grant, *The World of Rome,* p. 51.

p. 60 "Countless tribes": Lewis, *Roman Civilization,* p. 108.

p. 61 "Yes, even on holy": White, *Country Life in Classical Times,* p. 61.

p. 62 "Hither the farmer's": ibid., p. 100.

p. 63 "Put your hands": Shelton, *As the Romans Did,* p. 381.

INDEX

Page numbers for illustrations are in boldface.

agricultural and animal products, 5-6, **5**

Ambarvalia (holiday), 62, 63

Apuleius (author), 31

army, Roman, 6-9, **8**
    frontier forts, 16-17, **16**
    Roman rule and military occupation, 60

Augustus, emperor, 2

barbarian women, 50, **50**

bathhouse, 25, **25**

Boudicca, queen, 50

Calgacus (British leader), 8-9

Calpurnia (Pliny's wife), 47

children, Roman, **52**, 53-54
    born as slaves, 30, 51
    childbirth, 46-47, **46**, 51, 53, 54-55, **54**
    childhood, 55-57, **56**, **57**

Cincinnatus (farmer), 38

cities, Roman, 1, 2
    sustaining, 4-6, **5**

citizenship, Roman, 7

clothing, 19

Columella (architect), 26, 31, 38, 48-49, 51

countryside and rural life, viii, 1, 2, 4

communities, **10**, 11-17, **15**, **16**
    country homes, **18**, 19-27, **24**, **25**
    men of the soil, **36**, 37-43, **39**, **40**
    military conquests, 6-9, **8**
    poems about, 1, 3, 22-23, 32, 43, 48
    working the land, **28**, 29-35, **31**, **32**, **33**

Dio Cassius (historian), 50

Diodorus Siculus (historian), 35

diseases, illnesses, and injuries, 59-60

estates, country, 14-15, **14**, 49, 51

family, Roman, the father in, 37

farming, 2, 29
    agriculture and farm management, 38-39, 42
    crop failures, 59-60
    farmer-heroes, 38
    farmers and farmworkers, **36**, 37-38
    farms and farmhouses, 21
    holidays and celebrations, 61, 62
    seasonal cycle, 32-34, **32**, **33**
    slave labor, **28**, 30-31, **31**, 32, 48-49, 51
    tenant farmers, 15, 42-43, 48

festivals, Roman, 62-63

fishermen, 35

forewoman's duties, 49, 51

freeholders, 17, 40-41, **40**
frontier forts, 16-17, **16**

Galen (doctor), 59-60
games, children's, 56, **56**
German communities, 13
grain, 5
guardianship, 45

Hadrian, emperor, 15, 42
Hadrian's Wall, 16
herders, 34-35
holidays and celebrations, Roman,
    58, 61-63, **61**, **63**
homes, Roman country, **18**, 19-27,
    24, **25**
Horace (poet), 2, 15, 19, 24, 29, 37

imports and exports, Roman, 5-6

Jewish population, 12, 61

landowners
    large, 14-15
    leisurely, 38-39, **39**, 42

Marcus Aurelius (emperor), 29, 56-57
marriage, 46, 47
Martial (poet), 2, 6
milecastles, 16
mining, 35
musical instruments, **61**, **63**

nomads, 17

occupations, rural, viii, 1, 34-35, **35**
    see also farming
olive oil, 5, **33**, 34
Ovid (poet), 19, 22-23, 55, 59, 60,
    62, 63

Parilia (holiday), 62
Pliny the Younger, 2, 12, 25, 30-31,
    39, 42, 45-46, 47-48
procurators, 14

religious holidays, 61
Robigalia (holiday), 62-63
Romulus, 2

Seneca the Younger, 53
sharecroppers, 15, 43
shepherds, 48-49, **49**
slavery
    female slaves, 48-49, 51, 55
    holidays and celebrations, 61
    slave labor, 15, **28**, 30-31, **31**, 32

Tacitus (historian), 2, 7-9, 13, 50, 60
tenant farmers, 15, 42-43, 48
Terminalia (holiday), 62
Tibullus (poet), 2, 40, 45, 48, 56
Trajan, emperor, 16, 39

Varro, 34, 35, 48-49, 54

villages, 12, 16

villas, Roman, 6, **10**, 12, 24-27, **24**,
    25, **39**

vineyards, 5, 32, 33-34

Virgil (poet), 1, 2, 3, 11, 12, 29, 32,
    43, 61

Vitruvius (architect), 20

warfare, 60

women, rural, **44**, 45-46

    barbarian women, 50, **50**

    wives and mothers, 46-48, **46**, **47**

    working women, 48-49, **49**, 51

ABOUT THE AUTHOR

Fox Gradin, Celestial Studios Photography

KATHRYN HINDS grew up near Rochester, New York. In college she studied music and writing, and went on to do graduate work in comparative literature and medieval studies at the City University of New York. She has written a number of books for young people, including Benchmark Books' LIFE IN THE MIDDLE AGES series and LIFE IN THE RENAISSANCE series. Kathryn now lives in Georgia's Blue Ridge Mountains with her husband, their son, two dogs, and three cats. When she is not writing, she enjoys dancing, reading, playing music, and taking walks in the woods.